Dragon Chinese Horoscope 2024

By
IChingHun FengShuisu

Copyright © 2024 By IChingHun FengShuisu
All rights reserved

Table of Contents

Introduce 5
Year of the DRAGON (Gold) | (1940) & (2000) 7
   Overview 7
   Career and Business 10
   Financial 11
   Family 12
   Love 13
   Health 14
Year of the DRAGON (Water) | (1952) & (2012) 16
   Overview 16
   Career and Business 18
   Financial 20
   Family 21
   Love 21
   Health 22
Year of the DRAGON (Wood) | (1964) 24
   Overview 24
   Career and Business 25
   Financial 26
   Family 27
   Love 28
   Health 28
Year of the DRAGON (Fire) | (1976) 30
   Overview 30
   Career and Business 31
   Financial 32
   Family 33

- Love 34
- Health 35

Year of the DRAGON (Earth) | (1988) 37
- Overview 37
- Career and Business 38
- Financial 40
- Family 41
- Love 42
- Health 42

Chinese Astrology Horoscope for Each Month 44
- Month 12 in the Rabbit Year (6 Jan 24 - 3 Feb 24) 44
- Month 1 in the Dragon Year (4 Feb 24 - 5 Mar 24) 46
- Month 2 in the Dragon Year (6 Mar 24 - 5 Apr 24) 48
- Month 3 in the Dragon Year (6 Apr 24 - 5 May 24) 51
- Month 4 in the Dragon Year (6 May 24 - 5 Jun 24) 53
- Month 5 in the Dragon Year (6 Jun 24 - 6 Jul 24) 55
- Month 6 in the Dragon Year (7 Jul 24 - 7 Aug 24) 57
- Month 7 in the Dragon Year (8 Aug 24 - 7 Sep 24) 60
- Month 8 in the Dragon Year (8 Sep 24 - 7 Oct 24) 62
- Month 9 in the Dragon Year (8 Oct 24 - 6 Nov 24) 65
- Month 10 in the Dragon Year (7 Nov 24 - 6 Dec 24) 67
- Month 11 in the Dragon Year (7 Dec 24 - 5 Jan 24) 70

Amulet for The Year of the Dragon 73

Introduce

The character of people born in the year of the DRAGON

People born this year are sexy, cute, agile, and charming, and whoever sees them loves them. Popular perfection is also available. People born in the Year of the Dragon are self-assured. You are dynamic, influential, and quick. You have a strong and steadfast personality as well. People born in the Year of the Dragon enjoy talking, often have strong opinions, enjoy advising others, and produce excellent work. They are, however, angry and self-satisfied. Self-assurance is so strong that it is easily irritated, stubborn, authoritarian, and snobbish. Obsessed with position and money. People born in this year only have lovers. Always have faith in love. If he were a woman, young men would come almost every day to flirt with him.

Strength:
You are courageous and ambitious.
Weaknesses:

You are stubborn, and direct, and tend to do things that are beyond your control.

Love:
People born this year will be preoccupied with finding a partner or selecting a lover. You're not interested in his social standing or family. People enjoy accepting who their lover is. They are, indeed, very romantic. It also has a fascinating love mood in the stage that is sweet, and soft, and people born this year are often flirting, but it is a quiet flirt. However, it is capable of effective restraint. If it's a woman, she might pick the ugliest man to be her boyfriend. Like anything unusual. Similarly, if she's a man, she'll pick a girl who no one likes as her boyfriend. Strangely, his actions can completely occupy the hearts of lovers. When you have feelings for someone. You're always worried about it. You take care of your lover and will never break his or her heart.

Suitable Career:
Because people born in the year of the Dragon are earth elementals. As a result, a profession

destined for people born with your element is suitable for jobs related to soil and land, such as real estate. Trading in jade, stone, farming, farming, horticulture, livestock, feed industry, fertilizer, building materials, brokers, or full-time jobs that do not require movements, such as company employees, clerks, secretaries, administrative personnel, etc.

Year of the DRAGON (Gold) | (1940) & (2000)

"The DRAGON Fly" is a person born in the year of the DRAGON at the age of 84 years (1940) and 25 years (2000)

Overview

This year, the planet that orbits to spread its effect on the senior destined person is Dao Bun Chiang, helping your job to be wealthy and able to move ahead continually. However, this year has been influenced by your energy and your birth year. As a result, you should prioritize taking care of your physical health. Pay attention to eating well and getting adequate rest. When walking or engaging in other activities, you should use caution. You may feel dizzy, causing you to slip and fall. Furthermore, at the start of the year, you should be able to pay tribute to the god Tai Suai to fend against calamity. If traveling alone is inconvenient, you can carry an exorcism kit acquired from the firm or a temple to execute the "Kaliao" ceremony by bringing a set of paper offerings to brush oneself off. Then leave your children or close relatives to deposit them at the temple's designated location. To request blessings from the Tai Suai Buddha to assist in safeguarding the god from harm. Throughout the year, you may find quiet and tranquillity.

This year is regarded as another year in which all professional activities should not be impetuous and behave rashly for the youthful destinies of the Year of the Dragon. Before proceeding, you should consider carefully. This is because your birth year will coincide with another zodiac sign experiencing high energy, and you are also reaching a watershed moment in your life. As a result, you must have the bravery to face and embrace change, dare to think again, try new things, and never be neglectful in your actions. However, it is considered fortunate that the auspicious stars Bunchiang and Hokchae would arise and shine during the year of your destiny. As a result, part of the misery is mitigated. If your home can accommodate a variety of fortunate occasions this year. Auspicious energy can aid in the defeat of negative energy. However, if no auspicious occasion is taking place, you must be wary of the issues and obstructions that may arise as a result of the procession. The first is that disagreements and confrontations are common at home and work. Be cautious during the conclusion of the hot season and the start of the rainy season, since there will be troubles that will cause you to lose your fortune. You, too, must be extra cautious about accidents while at work and on the road. Bullies prefer to get in trouble and then bully you. To be safe, you need to know how to avoid it by using tenderness and force. You will only lose if you engage in a battle. People with a lot of patience will be able to get through difficult situations. These are all possibilities. As a result, at the start of the year, you should seek out a chance to pay your respects to the deity Tai Suai to ward off disaster and lighten your load.

Career and Business

This teenage fortune-teller's profession has taken off this year. Because you were born in a year that overlapped with your birth year. As a result, one should be wary of internal disagreements that might stymie growth. Even if fortunate stars appear to come to your aid, they can only provide partial assistance. You must, however, rely on your judgment and ability to get through this year. You can make progress if you truly set your mind to it. Don't just sit there and claim that working harder would put you at a disadvantage. Everyone's hard work will be noticed, and it will serve as a driving force to drive development toward a bright future. The 4th Chinese month (5 May - 4 Jun.), the 7th Chinese month (7 Aug. - 6 Sep.), the 8th Chinese month (7 Sep. - 7 Oct.) and the 11th Chinese month (6 Dec. '24 - 4 Jan '25) are the months in which your job or business will advance and develop. Concerning the months in which your employment and investments may face barriers and issues. The 12th Chinese month (6 Jan. - 3 Feb.), the 2nd Chinese month (5 Mar. - 3 Apr.), the 3rd Chinese month (4 Apr. - 4 May), and the Chinese 9th month (8 Oct. - 6 Nov.) are all included. You will make mistakes and inflict harm if you work carefully. Both have conditions for being duped or bullied, such as entering into job contracts. When asking for money or anything else, you must exercise greater caution to avoid being taken advantage of. Before signing the paper, you should carefully study the details. Furthermore, you should postpone investing during this time. Because you will face dangers and be duped by crooks.

Financial
This year's financial fortunes are favorable. Direct revenue is generally received. However, anyone who wishes to participate must incur their own risk because the outcome is unclear. You should be able to spend money wisely. Always strive to improve yourself regularly. Look for methods to earn more money. It will

benefit your money. During the month, keep an eye out for money leakage. Including unforeseen costs, such as the 12th Chinese month (6 Jan. - 3 Feb.), the 2nd Chinese month (5 Mar. - 3 Apr.), the 3rd Chinese month (4 Apr. - 4 May), and the 9th Chinese month (8 Oct. - 6 Nov.). Do not lend money or sign financial assurances for others. Do not gamble, invest in unlawful companies, or violate intellectual property rights. Because it will result in criminal penalties and the loss of a substantial chunk of money. For the months when your funds will run well, such as the 4th Chinese month (5 May. - 4 Jun.), the 7th Chinese month (7 Aug. - 6 Sep.), the 8th Chinese month (7 Sep. - 7 Oct.), and the 11th Chinese month (6 Dec. '24 - 4 Jan. '25).

Family

This year's family situation is not favorable. You should be wary of kids or staff causing problems in the residence. Maintaining bonds among family members is also important. Allow quarrels and quarrels to disrupt the tranquility in the home. Especially during the months when there will be extraordinary commotion in your family, such as the 12th Chinese month (6 Jan. - 3 Feb.), the 2nd Chinese month (5 Mar. - 3 Apr.), the Chinese 3rd month (4 Apr - 4 May) and the Chinese 9th month (8 Oct. - 6 Nov.), you should be especially cautious regarding home safety. Anything that is damaged should be fixed or replaced right away. You should also pay great attention to the health of the elderly in your home. Be wary of squabbles between persons in the house and those close. Avoid doing anything that may prevent the two houses from seeing one other. Furthermore, you must be cautious about valuables being destroyed, lost, or stolen.

Love

This year, you must pay more attention to your young destiny's love and connections. Although your loved ones will assist and support you in numerous ways. But, like watering the soil, love must be visited and cared for. The love tree will bloom and grow magnificently. However, you should be especially cautious during the 12th Chinese month (6 Jan. - 3 Feb.), the 2nd Chinese month (5 Mar. - 3 Apr.), the 3rd Chinese month (4 Apr. - 4 May), and the 9th Chinese month (8

Oct. - 6 Nov.), when love is particularly fragile and easily causes quarrels. Control your actions more tightly. Don't become so preoccupied with one item that it interferes with your main work or other aspects of your life. You should also avoid going to entertainment venues since it will lead the family to split up.

Health

This year's health outlook is bleak. It occurred because your health basis was surrounded by unlucky stars, who sent negative energy to you. You should take good care of your health and avoid becoming sick if you were born in both life cycles. Keep an eye out for contagious illnesses, outbreaks, and other mishaps. The 12th Chinese month (6 Jan. - 3 Feb.), the 2nd Chinese month (5 Mar. - 3 Apr.), the 3rd Chinese month (4 Apr. - 4 May), and the 9th Chinese month (8 Oct. - 6 Nov.) are all times when you should prioritize your health care. Avoid driving if you have consumed alcohol or intoxicants. Do not experiment with any medicines. Seniors must be more conscientious about self-care this year. Food must be clean and sanitary. Get enough rest and visit your doctor regularly to monitor your health. You should also keep a look out for physical anomalies. Be wary of ailments that appear to be trivial. However, if not addressed promptly, it might escalate into a major issue.

Year of the DRAGON (Water) | (1952) & (2012)

" The DRAGON swam in the rain " is a person born in the year of the DRAGON at the age of 72 years (1952) and 12 years (2012)

Overview

Even the planets that circle into your destined abode this year are "Hokchae stars" that orbit to support and encourage senior destinies around this age. However, this year has been influenced by the power of Khak and over the year of birth, as well as being plagued by a group of unfavorable stars. There will be various work activities that will take place, therefore one should not be impatient. Before taking action, you must first see clearly. Specifically, the capital issue. Both will incur significant costs. Including unanticipated current spending that leads your funds to be insufficiently liquid, producing issues in other areas. Health issues have the second largest impact. When walking, keep an eye out for high and low points. Dizziness from sickness, for example, might lead you to stumble, fall, and damage yourself. You must also be more cautious about traffic accidents and their consequences. You must exercise caution since you will suffer from the loss of your older family. As a result, you should look for a chance to pay tribute to the Thai gods at the start of the year to fend against calamity. If traveling alone is inconvenient, you can carry an exorcism kit acquired from the firm or a temple to execute the "Kaliao" ceremony by bringing a set of paper offerings to brush oneself off. Then leave your children or close relatives to deposit them at the temple's designated location. To request blessings from the Tai Suai Buddha to assist in safeguarding the god from harm. From heavy to mild relaxation

The planets that circle into the horoscope of the kid this year are "Dao Bun Chiang" for the young horoscope of the Year of the Dragon, even if his studies have progressed and can continue indefinitely. However, because it occurred in a year that overlapped the year of birth, it was also influenced by an evil star. If you do not increase your vigilance, children will be particularly interested in technology this year, and the temptations surrounding them will lead their minds to become scattered and unable to concentrate. As a result, one must exercise caution because this will result in poor academic achievement, which may lead to complications. Furthermore, parents should urge their children to be cautious while they are outside the home frequently. They must be cautious of incidents that might result in harm. Don't be irresponsible when traveling, participating in sports, or visiting foreign areas.

Career and Business

This year's efforts may encounter difficulties. This year is thus a wonderful moment for you to identify a successor or someone close to you to assist you in your career so that you can continue. It's because an evil star has infested the mansion of destiny. It will cause issues in internal and exterior confrontations, as well as the appearance of several hurdles. This year, we must be cautious of misunderstandings and orders that may result in a major disagreement with clients or business partners. The 12th Chinese month (6 Jan. - 3 Feb.), the 2nd Chinese month (5 Mar. - 3 Apr.), the 3rd Chinese month

(4 Apr. - 4 May), and the 9th Chinese month (8 Oct. - 6 Nov.) are the months where you should be extra careful and attentive in your job. If you face an issue anyplace, you should mediate to resolve it as soon as possible. Don't let things get out of hand. Furthermore, exercise greater caution while signing into job contracts or accepting employment. You should pay close attention to the specifics. This is not something you will have to deal with later. It is not a good time to form joint ventures or invest in many sectors during these months.

There are several challenges. Be wary about being duped or manipulated into losing money. You should be especially wary of anyone who invites you to join joint ventures or sign collaboration contracts. The months in which your job and company will move smoothly include the 4th Chinese month (5 May - 4 Jun.), the 7th Chinese month (7 Aug. - 6 Sep.), the 8th Chinese month (7 Sep. - 7 Oct.), and the 11th Chinese month (6 Dec. 2024 - 4 Jan. 25).

Financial

The financial prospects for this year are bleak. Income is down, while costs are rising in the background. Both will discover financial leaks, resulting in revenue that is insufficient to pay costs. You will also face huge unanticipated bills that will disrupt your plans and deplete your savings. Saving and spending wisely will be beneficial. You should not be eager for money you do not deserve, and you should avoid gambling. It will be enough to have a bit extra money in reserve. Especially during the months when finances are crucial and tough, such as the 12th Chinese month (6 Jan. - 3 Feb.), the 2nd Chinese month (5 Mar. - 3 Apr.), the 3rd Chinese month (4 Apr. - 4 May), and the 9th Chinese month (8 Oct. - 6 Nov.). During this time, avoid incurring new debt by lending money to others, signing financial guarantees, or being selfish. If you invest in a dangerous business inadvertently, the money you plan to make may be lost instead. For the month in which your finances improved. Including having some good fortune, including the 4th Chinese month (5 May - 4 Jun.), the 7th Chinese month (7 Aug. - 6 Sep.), the 8th Chinese month (7 Sep. – 7 Oct.), and the 11th Chinese month (6 Dec. '24 – 4 Jan. '25)

Family

This year's family requirements are poor. Because a swarm of wicked stars emerged and tormented them. This will extend its impact and lead individuals in the household to fall unwell regularly. You must also be cautious of unanticipated mishaps, and this year you may encounter misfortune and have to mourn for your old relatives. During the 12th Chinese month (6 Jan. - 3 Feb.), the 2nd Chinese month (5 Mar. - 3 Apr.), the 3rd Chinese month (4 Apr - 4 May), and the 9th Chinese month (8 Oct. - 6 Nov.) to take close care and attention to the elderly.

Love

This year's love connections are mild. This is a good year to take your spouse on a sightseeing tour to worship the Lord Buddha. Participate in merit-making and charitable events as well. It will aid in clearing your thoughts and positively resolving numerous issues. Dissatisfaction from the past should not be brought up again to be discussed. It will become a point of contention. Allow the matter that has passed to pass. Do not check for seams. Especially during the months when your love is quite fragile and problems can easily arise, including the 12th Chinese month (6 Jan. - 3 Feb.), the 2nd Chinese month (5 Mar. - 3 Apr.), 3rd Chinese month (4 Apr. - 4 May) and 9th Chinese month (8 Oct. - 6 Nov.).

Health

The elder destined person's health is not excellent this year because the destined home faces both the malevolent star Sung Mung (gate of death) and the star Tiao Khae (funeral visitor). As a result, whatever you do, you should not be inattentive or careless about the hazards of illness and sickness, as well as numerous mishaps. more during the months when you need to be more severe and sensitive to taking care of yourself, such as the 12th Chinese month (6 Jan. - 3 Feb.), the 2nd Chinese month (5 Mar. - 3 Apr.), the 3rd Chinese month (4 Apr. - 4 May), and the 9th Chinese month (8 Oct. - 6 Nov.). Be cautious of the possibility of harm when riding in an automobile for young kids. While participating in various activities or playing, be cautious of drinking and eating filthy food, which can result in contagious illnesses or food poisoning.

Year of the DRAGON (Wood) | (1964)

"The Dragon in Ocean" is a person born in the year of the DRAGON at the age of 60 years (1964)

Overview

Because the Year of the Dragon corresponds with your birth year, persons born in this year will be roughly 60 years old. Furthermore, your birth year is a zodiac sign that will be influenced by the Tai Suai element. It was like an assault on Ong Tai Suai's skull. Furthermore, the mansion of destiny was visited by a swarm of unfortunate stars circling to destroy and torment. As a result, health issues will be the first to affect you. Keep an eye out for high blood pressure, heart disease, hepatitis, and vascular issues. As a result, this year, you should pay close attention to any changes in your body. Both should get annual physicals regularly. If something unusual is discovered, it will be handled as soon as possible. Furthermore, you should be cautious of the possibility of harm and bleeding from slips and falls or accidents. As a result, you cannot afford to be irresponsible about accidents this year, whether at work or on the road. Money, employment, and family issues will come next. It will result in work and business not being completed or goals not being met. Choosing to engage in diverse activities requires extreme caution to avoid mistakes and damage. Unexpected losses will result from your financial fortunes. You should not anticipate a windfall. There will be strife and confusion in the household. However, a fortunate star emerged throughout the year. "Buen Chiang" circles to spread good fortune.

Career and Business

This year's job sector, particularly commercial enterprise, has been hit by a rainstorm. You will face several challenges. You must also use caution in selecting the appropriate personnel for the proper position. Don't hire someone who can't do the job. It will wreak havoc on the work. You must find a career that is appropriate for your abilities because relying on others this year may not be what you desire. Especially during the months when work and company will face several challenges, such as the 12th Chinese month (6 Jan.- 3 Feb.), the 2nd Chinese month (5 Mar. - 3 Apr.), the 3rd Chinese month (4 Apr. - 4 May) and the 9th Chinese month (8 Oct - 6 Nov). You should be cautious when interacting with or communicating with clients during these months. Those who need to run errands are included. Because a lack of clear communication leads to severe blunders that can affect other problems. In terms of signing different contract agreements.

Financial

The financial fortunes of this year are highly variable. It is because the cumulative power of the year affects it. Direct cash flow is OK, but windfall is not. If you want to give it a go, you must be ready to do so at your own risk. Both should be wary of economic swings both within and beyond the country. It will have an impact on the company's loss. Accounting mistakes should also be avoided if they are not thoroughly investigated and followed up on. Especially during months with financial leaks and unanticipated costs, such as the 12th Chinese month (6 Jan. - 3 Feb.), the 2nd Chinese month (5 Mar. - 3 Apr.)., the 3rd Chinese month (4 Apr. - 4 May), and the 9th Chinese month (8 Oct - 6 Nov). You should not be greedy and invest in firms that are dangerous to the country's laws. Because there is a considerable risk of a lawsuit at this time, it is prohibited to gamble, lend money to others, or sign financial commitments.

Family

This year has been a difficult one for the family. You must be wary of subordinates who cause problems. It is because the chosen individual has witnessed the power of producing together. As a result, if you have the opportunity, pay homage to the Tai Suai Buddha at the start of the year to fend off ill luck. It's sufficient to alleviate the pain. However, in the next months, you must be more cautious and prepared. The 12th Chinese month (6 Jan. - 3 Feb.), the 2nd Chinese month (5 Mar. - 3 Apr.), the 3rd Chinese month (4 Apr. - 4 May), and the 9th month of China (8 Oct. - 6 Nov.) will be very chaotic within the household. You will most certainly lose possessions as well as medical bills for yourself and the people in your house.

You should also be wary of crooks or thieves breaking into your house.

Love

The love aspect is not favorable since you will experience mood swings and become angry more quickly this year. Another reason is that you frequently lack control over your emotions, which makes things simple. As a result, you should exercise caution during the following months, which are prone to causing quarrels and rifts in marital life: the 12th Chinese month (6 Jan. - 3 Feb.), the 2nd Chinese month (5 Mar. - 3 Apr.), the 3rd Chinese month (4 Apr. - 4 May), and the 9th Chinese month (8 Oct. - 6 Nov.). During this time, avoid acting as a third party in other people's families' relationships and avoid going to various entertainment places.

Health

The selected person's physical health is not excellent this year. This is because the wicked stars that have infiltrated your destiny have impacted your health basis this year. As a result, you should be wary of past ailments reappearing as well as silent disorders that may endanger you. You should also be on the lookout for heart disease, liver disease, high blood pressure, and blood vessel issues. You should pay extra attention to your physical health over the following months, including the 12th Chinese month (6 Jan. - 3 Feb.), the 2nd Chinese month (5 Mar. - 3 Apr.), the 3rd Chinese month (4 Apr. - 4 May) and the 9th Chinese month (8 Oct.- 6 Nov.) You should keep a watch out for any irregularities in your body. In addition, you should see your doctor regularly for an annual health check. You should also reduce your intake of sugary, fatty, and salty meals. Don't go too far. Because it has the potential to exacerbate a variety of infectious disorders. You should be cautious when venturing out this year. When driving, you should be cautious about accidents.

Year of the DRAGON (Fire) | (1976)

" The DRAGON in hibernation" is a person born in the year of the DRAGON at the age of 48 years (1976)

Overview

This is because the Year of the Dragon corresponds with the year of birth for people born around this time. Furthermore, his birth year is considered another zodiac sign influenced by the Tai Suai god. Your life's journey has been rocky. Throughout the year, you will have difficulties and upheaval that you will have to deal with daily. And you'll have to utilize more strength and management than usual to go through each subject. As a result, in living your life and making judgments in numerous areas this year, you should be calm and prudent. Before taking any action, assess the surrounding situation to ensure your safety. In terms of people, one must be cautious of potential conflicts, whether within the agency or over the administrative line. If you accomplish nothing this year, nothing will change. However, it will increase and cause tiny things to become large. As a result, this year, if there is an issue, you should find a solution as soon as possible. Because leaving it ignored for too long will harm the overall picture. In terms of health, be wary of lurking threats that will make you uncomfortable. So, if you have unpleasant symptoms or feel weird in your body this year, I couldn't be complacent. You should consult a doctor right away for a diagnosis and treatment.

Career and Business

This year's work was hampered by rain. The effort and outcomes will not be as fulfilling as a tiger-headed snake-tailed monster. You should also exercise caution in controlling your thoughts and not allowing your emotions to become unconscious. Because it may result in work being harmed or a lapse in words that are not as agreed upon, which would erode credibility and disgrace oneself, whose reputation has not grown in only a day or two. As a result, you should avoid making mistakes, particularly during the 12th Chinese month (6 Jan. - 3 Feb.), the 2nd Chinese month (5 Mar. - 3 Apr.), the 3rd Chinese month (4 Apr. - 4 May), and the 9th Chinese month (8 Oct. - 6 Nov.). Be wary of ambiguous messages. You may sustain harm. It should also be avoided if the contract conditions you must sign place you at a significant disadvantage. It is preferable to decline. To begin a new employment, buy stocks, and make different investments. This year is an important factor to consider before investing. Because there is a good probability the investment may vanish before your eyes. There is a chance of being duped by a partner or having your account robbed, causing you harm. However, there are certain months this year when your work and business will return easily and prosperously, like the 4th Chinese month (5 May - 4 Jun.), the 7th Chinese month (7 Aug. - 6 Jul.), the 8th Chinese month (7 Sep.- 7 Oct.), and the 11th Chinese month (6 Dec. '24 - 4 Jan. '25).

Financial

This year's financial fortunes are not going as well as planned. It is frequently discovered that present expenditures are consuming liquidity or that there are damages that must be pursued to recompense others. As a result, at the start of the year, you might buy goods you want to avoid the misfortune of losing money too soon. Especially if you enter the following months, which can cause leaks in your money and cause goods to go missing, notably the 12th Chinese month (6 Jan. - 3 Feb.), the 2nd Chinese month (5 Mar. - 3 Apr.), the 3rd Chinese month (4 Apr. - 4 May), and the 9th Chinese month (8 Oct. - 6 Nov.). Take caution not to become engaged in or invest in illegal companies or copyright infringement. Don't be avaricious. It will aid in the reduction of losses. Also, avoid gambling, lending money to others, and signing financial commitments. The months when your finances will return to normal are the 4th Chinese month (5 May - 4 Jun.), the 7th Chinese month (7 Aug. - 6 Sep.), the 8th Chinese month (7 Sep.- 7 Oct.), and the 11th Chinese month (6 Dec. '24 - 4 Jan '25).

Family

This year, families must exercise extreme caution. This is because the evil star Teo Khae (the funeral guest star) looks to be on his way to destroy the family base. As a result, one should be extremely cautious regarding family members' health issues, safety issues or accidents, and the dangers of mourning for senior relatives. The months in which the family will encounter exceptional turbulence are the 12th Chinese month (6 Jan. - 3 Feb.), the 2nd Chinese month (5 Mar. - 3 Apr.), the 3rd Chinese month (4 Apr. - 4 May), and the 9th Chinese month (8 Oct. - 6 Nov.). Take care of the health and safety of all family members, including tiny children and adults. Be wary of being duped by fraudsters into losing or damaging your belongings, or of criminals coming into and stealing things in your house.

Love

This year's love of the Lord of Destiny is not going well. Because it is the Year of the Pig, and devils are attempting to bother you. As a result, you are frequently in an unstable mood, easily annoyed, and irritable. So it appears that the other party will assist you. You are dissatisfied, frequently sparking confrontations over little to major issues. You should also exercise good emotional and behavioral control this year. Avoid becoming frivolous or engaging in seductions and vices. Because it's difficult to accept inappropriate behavior from someone you care about. During the months when your love is particularly weak and disputes are common, such as the 12th Chinese month (6 Jan. - 3 Feb.), and the 2nd Chinese month (5 Mar. - 3 Apr.). The Chinese third month (4 Apr. - 4 May) and the 9th Chinese month (8 Oct - 6 Nov). Avoid getting engaged in other people's relationships. Seeking enjoyment at entertainment venues will disrupt the family's harmony.

Health

This year's fate is in poor physical health. Three bad stars come to annoy you due to the state of your health: the Hokchi star, the Kao Sua star, and the Tiao Khae star. It is considered to harm the owner of fate in a variety of areas, including physical health issues. Be wary of concealed ailments or ones that frequently make you sick. You, too, must be cautious of being injured in an accident. The 12th Chinese month (6 Jan. - 3 Feb.), the 2nd Chinese month (5 Mar. - 3 Apr.), the 3rd Chinese month (4 Apr. - 4 May) and China's 9th month (8 Oct. - 6 Nov.) are the months to pay special attention to your health. Also, if there is a social event and the use of intoxicants during this time, you should not drive a car.

Year of the DRAGON (Earth) | (1988)

"The Dragon In Heaven" is a person born in the year of the DRAGON at the age of 36 years (1988)

Overview

Even though the planet that circles into your designated house this year is Bun Chiang, it falls in the year that coincides with the year of birth for the Year of the Dragon slated for this age cycle. The Chinese name it Huam, which is considered an insult to the Tai Suea's head. There appear to be many wicked stars in the house of destiny that come to focus on and upset, all of which will result in various challenges, issues, and obstacles. Throughout the year, you will encounter challenges and solve problems. There is a risk of losing money in terms of financial fortune. However, having an auspicious star blazing with support and assistance is still regarded as fortunate. There will be a way forward despite being surrounded by issues and impediments. This year, you must demonstrate dedication, effort, endurance, and strong interpersonal skills to others around you. This year's effort, on the other hand, cannot be greedy. However, you should investigate the true scenario. This work will result in either issues or positive outcomes. You should cease doing that task if adding, subtracting, multiplying, and dividing does not provide satisfactory results. How can you select a bad route over a good one if you're simply searching for a tiny current income while passing up the possibility of massive earnings in the future? As a result, to be successful this year, you need to cultivate positive connections inside the organization. There will be opportunities for job transfers, employment changes, promotions, and position changes throughout the year. However, if you have a good connection with your employer, he or she will encourage you. Colleagues will be there for you. You will have the opportunity to take a positive step forward.

Career and Business

This year will be a challenge in terms of work. You should do your job obligations to the best of your ability. Along with maintaining strong ties with those you must contact and always growing yourself. Be cautious of communication, whether at the upper or lower levels, especially during the months when you need to pay more attention because there will be a lot of problems and obstacles in your career, namely the 12th Chinese month (6 Jan. - 3 Feb.), the 2nd Chinese month (5 Mar. - 3 Apr.), the Chinese 3rd month (4 Apr - 4 May), and the Chinese 9th month (8 Oct. - 6 Nov.). Maintain your humility and respect for your elders. Adults will be kind and helpful. For the months in which your business and commerce will advance and thrive, such as the 4th Chinese month (5 May - 4 Jun), and the 7th Chinese month (7 Au. - 6 Sep.). , the 8th Chinese month (7 Sep.- 7 Oct.), and the 11th Chinese month (6 Dec '24 - 4 Jan '25). In terms of commencing a new employment. This year, you should exercise caution while investing in equities. Because there is a potential that a cheater or fraudster will attend an event or join a joint venture. The main element is to consider your readiness. If the capital you wish to invest in must be borrowed, don't do it, and don't prioritize tiny rewards above losing a significant quantity of money.

Financial

In terms of financial fortunes this year, loopholes, leakage spots, poor revenue, and exorbitant costs were discovered. You will see that your spending matches your income. Saving money is the most effective approach to assist. You should carefully arrange your spending. Also, avoid incurring additional debt and gambling. Do not invest in illegal or pirated businesses during the months when your finances will be tight and lacking liquidity, such as the 12th Chinese month (6 Jan. - 3 Feb., the 2nd Chinese month (5 Mar. - 3 Apr.), the 3rd Chinese month (4 Apr. - 4 May), and the 9th Chinese month (8 Oct. - 6 Nov.). You should not lend or sign to others at this time. Your finances will return to normal within the month. Including the 4th Chinese month (5 May - 4 Jun.), the 7th Chinese month (7 Aug. - 6 Sep.), the 8th Chinese month (7 Sep. - 7 Oct.), and the 11th Chinese month (6 Dec. '24 - 4 Jan. '25).

Family

The family requirements for this year are not excellent. This is due to the appearance of the wicked stars Kuangji and the stars throughout the year. This will lead to a slew of issues. What you should be cautious about is home security. The prevalence of quarrels within the house and confrontations with surrounding households. The 12th Chinese month (6 Jan. - 3 Feb.), the 2nd Chinese month (5 Mar. - 3 Apr.), the 3rd Chinese month (4 Apr. Sept. - 4 May), and the 9th Chinese month (8 Oct. - 6 Nov.) are the months when your house will be chaotic. You should be cool and accept it throughout this time. Make an effort to foster understanding and togetherness in the household. You must be fair to all parties as an adult. Always urge everyone to be courteous to their neighbors. Don't brag or act like a thug. You should also check the house's fixtures to determine if they are in excellent shape. If they are damaged, they should be fixed or replaced as soon as possible so that no one in the house is harmed.

Love

Due to the influence of malicious stars, there will be monsoon waves this year for the love of the Year of the Dragon.

Focusing on Guang Ji and the bad star Pua Bai, which exudes influence, would cause the destined person to become grumpy, easily annoyed, and furious. Your emotions are out of control. Your thoughts are perplexed and distrustful. As a result, you must exercise caution, particularly during the 12th Chinese month (6 Jan. - 3 Feb.), the 2nd Chinese month (5 Mar. - 3 Apr.), the 3rd Chinese month (4 Apr. - 4 May), and the 9th Chinese month (8 Oct. - 6 Nov.). You attempt to be patient and calm throughout this period. Things will settle down and improve if you take a step back. You must exercise caution in controlling your actions. Don't be deceived by the brilliant lights of going out to see shows. Because they risk contracting the sickness and causing family strife.

Health

The health horoscope for this year is bleak. You will suffer from allergies or develop an immune weakness. As a result, you must work to boost your immunity. Otherwise, I'm afraid you'll have to spend a lot of money on medical expenditures this year. You should also be cautious of automobile accidents when driving on the road. Especially during the months of the 12th Chinese month (6 Jan. - 3 Feb.), the 2nd Chinese month (5 Mar. - 3 Apr.), the 3rd Chinese month (4 Apr. - 4 May), and the 9th Chinese month (8 Oct. - 6 Nov.). To be healthy, you should take care of your body by exercising frequently and obtaining adequate sleep.

Chinese Astrology Horoscope for Each Month

Month 12 in the Rabbit Year (6 Jan 24 - 3 Feb 24)

When this month arrives, the fate of people born in the Year of the Dragon indicates negative energy. There is also a swarm of evil stars orbiting the fate graph, forcing it to plummet vertically. Various issues and contradictions emerged. You should also be wary of children or subordinates causing damage or malfunctions, which would hold you jointly liable. What you should do this month is be cool and composed while progressively seeking the fundamental reason and moving quickly to repair it immediately and decisively. During this time, there are both little and major issues and disruptions in the workplace, including business. Emotion cannot be used to judge many issues. Because you cannot control all external conditions, certain tasks must be delayed. Both must be prepared to deal with filling the holes. Be wary of wicked persons who are plotting to harm and ruin you from behind your back. You should also check your account frequently. Be wary of subordinates who are considering embezzlement or corruption. Contract documentation must also be properly prepared. To avoid falling for the fraudsters' techniques and causing harm.

This month is not going well financially. There will always be factors that cause you to spend money. You should never lend money or sign financial assurances to anyone. Avoid gambling, gambling, speculating, and engaging in unlawful transactions.

The family horoscope is a tumultuous situation. Keep an eye out for valuables that have been damaged, misplaced, or stolen. Be cautious about injuries sustained in the house.

In terms of love, everything has returned to normal. There's nothing to be concerned about.

In terms of health, you should practice good food hygiene and avoid having air allergies. Sleeping well will be hampered if you have a cold or are under stress.

For starting a new job, entering stocks, and making various investments. This month is not good and should be avoided.

Support Days: 1 Jan., 5 Jan., 9 Jan., 13 Jan., 17 Jan., 21 Jan., 25 Jan., 29 Jan.
Lucky Days: 10 Jan., 22 Jan.
Misfortune Days: 11 Jan., 23 Jan.
Bad Days: 2 Jan., 4 Jan., 14 Jan., 16 Jan., 26 Jan. , 28 Jan

Month 1 in the Dragon Year (4 Feb 24 - 5 Mar 24)
Even if your destiny graph looks to be heading higher, there are criteria for your destiny while entering this month. However, it appears that the accumulating difficulties have not been remedied. This month, you should prioritize your difficulties and work quickly to resolve any hurdles that are impeding the implementation of various initiatives. Build friendships and business ties with genuineness. To wait for a proper moment and chance to enter again. By gathering investment dollars and developing a human resource foundation,

you will be able to go forward and achieve your goal.

This month's work is generally better. The commercial business, for example, can proceed as usual. Even along the journey, you must solve difficulties and attempt to put an end to them. However, you must be vigilant and persistent. Increase sales by accelerating work production. Furthermore, this month you may invest and expand in a variety of areas to help your money grow. As a result, as the water rises, you must scoop it immediately. Even if some water escapes, you must accept it. But don't be a slacker and let wonderful possibilities pass you by. The pay for this wealth varies substantially. The expected income is still unknown. Gambling and fortune-telling still involve some risk. As a result, you must use caution. Another thing to be cautious about. Try to handle your limited operating cash to the best of your skills. Do not be greedy and expect money to be earned in an unethical and unlawful manner.

There is greater peace and harmony inside the family. The meaning is understood by the members of the home. The romantic aspect is strong. It's an exciting moment. Your husband and lover will be of great assistance and support to both of you. In terms of health, you should be cautious of stomach disease, intestinal sickness, and food poisoning.

Support Days: 2 Feb., 6 Feb., 10 Feb., 14 Feb., 18 Feb., 22 Feb., 26 Feb.
Lucky Days: 3 Feb., 15 Feb., 27 Feb
Misfortune Days: 4 Feb., 16 Feb., 28 Feb
Bad Days: 7 Feb., 9 Feb., 19 Feb., 21 Feb.

Month 2 in the Dragon Year (6 Mar 24 - 5 Apr 24)
Beginning this month, those born in the Year of the Dragon are categorized as a different zodiac sign. As a result, the house of fate will suffer ups and downs. To fend off ill luck and address troubles, the destined one should make time to pay reverence to the Tai Suai Buddha. Make merit and give regularly. It will be seen as building merit for a successful start. This month, you should make clear goals, plan your

work, and gather resources. There are funds and staff available. Just waiting for the appropriate timing and chance to go forward completely.

However, in terms of fortune, this pay has a proclivity to deplete money. As a result, you should save and spend wisely. Do not indulge in gambling or gambling out of greed. You should also avoid investing in illicit trade firms. To avoid a shortage of liquidity in your financial system, you need to know how to refuse to lend money or sign financial guarantees.

It is the seat of monsoons in terms of labor and trade. Management and the command line will have conflicts. Creating and strengthening solid relationships in both top and lower-level departments is what you should accomplish. To prevent conflict difficulties, one should not meddle or intervene in the tasks of others.

There are still unresolved issues about the family's riches. You must address problems caused by relatives, friends, and subordinates.

Valuables should be stored safely. Don't be greedy if you don't want to fall victim to fraudsters.

This month is easy on the heart. People who love one another and are attentive and persistent in looking after them can ask each other to make merit or go to faraway regions. It will help to deepen the love relationship. In terms of health, one must also be cautious of infectious diseases caused by overindulgent eating, as well as accidents caused by driving on the road.

Support Days: 1 Mar, 5 Mar., 9 Mar., 13 Mar., 17 Mar., 21 Mar., 25 Mar., 29 Mar.
Lucky Days: 10 Mar, 22 Mar.
Misfortune Days: 11 Mar, 23 Mar.
Bad Days: 2 Mar, 4 Mar., 14 Mar., 16 Mar., 26 Mar., 28 Mar.

Month 3 in the Dragon Year (6 Apr 24 - 5 May 24)

This month, the horoscope of people born in the Year of the Dragon has moved into the dangerous zone, leading the zodiac house to lose its equilibrium. Things that have been burning will erupt, causing upheaval. What you should do this month is know how to help clients or company partners who need to be contacted when difficulties emerge. Do not put off or postpone things to squander time. However, you must assume responsibility and deliver excellent service to keep people coming back for more.

In terms of business and business, you will face disagreements and pressures both inside and outside of various activities during this period. As a result, you should proceed with caution at all times. Also, do not interfere with the tasks of others. You should prioritize your tasks. There was no offside or overprotection. To avoid errors, while ordering or receiving work, it should be conveyed explicitly.

In terms of fortune, this wage is not favorable. Income is decreasing, and costs are catching up. If you continue to spend lavishly, funds will flow out and there may be a lack of liquidity. Furthermore, you should avoid holding receptions. Including a variety of stories about huge faces and big hearts. Avoid gaming to minimize needless losses. You should also avoid lending money to others or signing any commitments.

The family's horoscope is still up in the air. Take precautions to ensure your family's safety at home. Maintain strong relationships with your neighbors. Be wary of valuables in your home being misplaced or stolen. This era is like a hurricane in terms of love. Whatever you do, you should respect each other so that disagreements do not arise. In terms of health, you should still be cautious about accidents. This might result in hand or limb harm. This month is not favorable for starting a new career, buying stocks, or making other investments.

Support Days: 2 Apr., 6 Apr., 10 Apr., 14 Apr., 18 Apr., 22 Apr., 26 Apr., 30 Apr.
Lucky Days: 3 Apr., 15 Apr., 27 Apr
Misfortune Days: 4 Apr., 16 Apr., 28 Apr
Bad Days: 7 Apr., 9 Apr., 19 Apr., 21 Apr.

Month 4 in the Dragon Year (6 May 24 - 5 Jun 24)
This month, the fate criteria are expected to be more prosperous. Because the zodiac house shifts to experience the month that supports it as an ally. Immediately, the fortunate star Buon Chiang Chai was discovered blazing. The power of patronage therefore fosters the smooth running of work and business. What you should do this month is to dare to endure. Work hard, work light, and don't worry. It's called speeding the generation of outcomes. Increase sales and revenue from the beginning of the year.

This remuneration is generous in terms of wealth. The funds are still being received. Whatever you put money into before this era will pay off handsomely. It is also a favorable moment, an opportune chance for you to take action to advance your career or invest in your goals. The more diligent you are, the more you improve yourself, the greater your money will be. In terms of commerce, this is an exciting moment to enter the market and discover new clients, accelerate sales, increase the production base, and generate results by offering new projects so that work may progress and be able to raise the level to the next level.

The family prosperity is calm, and auspicious patronage is abundant. You will meet family and friends who are all working together. You will also make new acquaintances who will assist you in navigating professional pathways and introduce you to new consumers. Improve the efficiency of trade work

The loving side is as vivid as a fish taking in water. People who love and care for their hearts under all circumstances.

In terms of health, both the body and mind are in good shape and have enough energy to move on. To begin a new employment, buy stocks, and make different investments. This month is ideal for making investments in new market enterprises. You will receive a hefty payout at the end of the year if you so want.

Support Days: 4 May., 8 May., 12 May., 16 May., 20 May., 24 May., 28 May.
Lucky Days: 9 May., 21 May.
Misfortune Days: 10 May., 22 May.
Bad Days: 1 May., 3 May., 13 May., 15 May., 25 May., 27 May.

Month 5 in the Dragon Year (6 Jun 24 - 6 Jul 24)
The fortunes of people born in the Year of the Dragon have turned upside down as we enter this month. Life's path is paved with bad stars. Even if my heart is still fighting, my strength is insufficient. The difficulties and issues are more serious than normal. Things to remember at this period are: Don't forget about your former work. Don't try a new job. If you make a mistake, you will be heartbroken. In terms of work and business in this era, in addition to issues with administrative tasks, subordinates may split apart and move to work elsewhere. It

is a major waste of the organization's human resources. However, you must treat all employees fairly and equally in the workplace. Furthermore, you should use greater caution when signing contracts or paperwork. Be wary of contract provisions that may result in disadvantages or damage.

This wage is not excellent in terms of fortune. You may incur unforeseen bills that will deplete your savings. As a result, you should not enhance your risk by gambling or participating in any form of stock lottery. You should also avoid investing in illicit activities. Because being overly greedy might lead to the loss of your money. There might be criminal charges. There will be upheaval and conflict inside the family. Be wary of geriatric health issues and disagreements that create harm among family members. Be wary about having your things damaged, misplaced, or stolen.

This month's love horoscope predicts that a third party will intervene to provoke a split.

This month, be cautious of heart disease and excessive blood pressure, and always prioritize safety when traveling.

For starting a new career, buying stocks, and making different investments. This month's forecast is bleak and should be postponed or avoided for the time being.

Support Days: 1 Jun., 5 Jun., 9 Jun., 13 Jun., 17 Jun., 21 Jun., 25 Jun., 29 Jun
Lucky Days: 2 Jun., 14 Jun., 26 Jun
Misfortune Days: 3 Jun., 15 Jun., 27 Jun
Bad Days: 6 Jun., 8 Jun., 18 Jun., 20 Jun., 30 Jun.

Month 6 in the Dragon Year (7 Jul 24 - 7 Aug 24)
The fate requirements for persons born in the Year of the Dragon remain in the monsoon direction this month. The cumulative issues remain murky and appear to be escalating. Work and business problems will generate fresh stories. The same problems reoccur to be fixed, and new problems crop up until you barely have any spare time. What you should do this month is prioritize the major concerns.

Don't be casual and ignore it since it will become a hazard later. Furthermore, you should establish relationships with coworkers in the agency to learn how to operate as a team so that you are not left alone.

You may have to rush through your job tasks to continue and complete the old work properly, and you must keep modesty. You must also establish positive connections with your coworkers, as well as with customers and anyone with whom you come into touch. To make it easier to solve various difficulties.

This salary horoscope is sufficient. If you want to gain money from fortune, you must exercise caution. Because that might be the criteria. It is not the only item you will receive. You must also be cautious of unanticipated working cash outflows. As a result, while revenue is flowing in, you should carefully manage your expenditures to avoid a shortage of liquidity.

There is harmony throughout the family. Love's destiny is like being given a fresh start. Please be courageous enough to reconcile or to beg for love, and your request will be granted. It is also a health requirement to be cautious of accidents when at work and traveling. This month, you should be cautious of injuries caused by fractured bones or unintentional stumbles and falls. The fortunes of your family will improve because you will meet acquaintances who will assist you in resolving your employment dilemma.

Starting a new career, buying stocks, and making other investments are all options. This month, if you can do so, you will discover fresh and exciting investing opportunities.

Support Days: 3 Jul., 7 Jul., 11 Jul., 15 Jul., 19 Jul., 23 Jul., 27 Jul., 31 Jul.
Lucky Days: 8 Jul., 20 Jul.
Misfortune Days: 9 Jul., 21 Jul.
Bad Days: 2 Jul., 12 Jul., 14 Jul., 24 Jul., 26 July.

Month 7 in the Dragon Year (8 Aug 24 - 7 Sep 24)

This month, the path of people born in the Year of the Dragon takes an appropriate turn. As a result, the horoscope's orientation is changing. The way started to lighten. Things that are an impediment and cause concern will be identified at this stage, and a solution will be found. What you should do this month is use the information and experience gained from prior mistakes as a benefit and guidance for completing activities ahead of time, when many things are already well prepared. During this month, you can activate the green light and accelerate your engine to get moving right away. What you should not overlook is the need to maintain and strengthen connections with those around you regularly, especially if a good opportunity presents itself. You must make a choice and muster the confidence to act. Because if you don't have enough guts, you will lack it. It is the same as passing up an opportunity for growth.

During this time, you will find the power of development and wealth in your career and trade. Your labor will be rewarded with both money and renown. Because stars will help and encourage you if you enhance your dedication and patience. Never stop learning and growing as a person. There will be an opportunity to obtain what you desire. So, be resolute, don't be disheartened, and don't be misled by others; instead, keep moving forward to achieve your goal. This salary horoscope is the best spot to get rich. As a result, you should concentrate on earning a livelihood, and work more, and your earnings will rise.

The fortunes of the family are serene, and fortunate energy has arrived at the house. Love's fate reaches a crossroads where decisions must be taken. You should think hard about whether you want to move ahead or backward. If you genuinely love someone and want to marry them, go ahead and ask for their love. Otherwise, you might not be able to travel where you want.

This month's horoscope for family and friends is favorable. If you get stuck, you will be helped.

Both will receive advice or have appropriate functioning guidelines.

There are strong prospects to invest and move forward with the company this month for establishing a new job, joining stocks, and making other investments.

Support Days: 4 Aug., 8 Aug., 12 Aug., 16 Aug., 20 Aug., 24 Aug., 28 Aug.
Lucky Days: 1 Aug., 13 Aug., 25 Aug.
Misfortune Days: 2 Aug., 14 Aug. ., 26 Aug
Bad Days: 5 Aug., 7 Aug., 17 Aug., 19 Aug., 29 Aug., 31 Aug.

Month 8 in the Dragon Year (8 Sep 24 - 7 Oct 24)
This month's horoscope is more positive. It is reported that the skies intervened and cleared the path for you once more. The physical and mental power required is not in vain. Even if you do a lot, it is still a criterion for earning a well-deserved prize. As a result, if you battle without giving up, you must improve your diligence and endurance to withstand the

friction of your luck. The higher the probability that the response will be a good number. This month, you should improve and alter to stay up with market trends. Plan and prepare your work.

Enter at the appropriate time and location. When the right moment arrives, you'll be able to make a lot of money.

In terms of business and commerce, this time demonstrates the strength of support and promotion. If you have an excellent strategy or project for this event, act quickly. Because it will assist in ensuring that numerous processes run smoothly throughout a smooth period. It was a successful period for business. You might opt to expand by investing in numerous businesses. Please be vigilant in your quest for knowledge. Examine the issue in conjunction with your purpose and boost your confidence in investing. Don't allow a wonderful chance to pass you by without seizing it.

This is a respectable pay for wealth. What you have invested will generate cash inflows. Please be determined to move on and grab any further possibilities that present themselves. Then you will sit and count the money as an encouraging present. This month, you may hear wonderful news from your relatives. It might be about the success of the individuals in the house. Family members are forgiving and prepared to make adjustments. Help and support are provided by family and friends.

The love horoscope for this month is good. You can propose, become engaged, marry, and marry again. Anyone who is still unmarried does not want to go to bed alone. An excellent opportunity has presented itself to you at this moment. If you wish to inquire, please do so as soon as possible. No need to be concerned about your health. The body is in good physical and mental health.

Support Days: 1 Sep., 5 Sep., 9 Sep., 13 Sep., 17 Sep., 21 Sep., 25 Sep., 29 Sep.
Lucky Days: 6 Sep., 18 Sep. , 30 Sep
Misfortune Days: 7 Sep., 19 Sep.
Bad Days: 10 Sep., 12 Sep., 22 Sep., 24 Sep.

Month 9 in the Dragon Year (8 Oct 24 - 6 Nov 24)
Those born in the Year of the Dragon this month will experience a cancerous trend in their lives. Your fate has taken a terrible turn. The seething unease will eventually burst forth. This month, make sure that every work activity is carried out following the norms and etiquette and remember that only those who know how to respect others will be respected. Make no rash judgments or act rashly this month. Because if you make a mistake, you may face a bleak future.

During this time, there will be problems at work and in management. You should be mindful of your posture and language while interacting with coworkers and bosses. Also, do not interrupt or intervene in the tasks of others. Making contracts or signing work paperwork, for example, to boost completeness. Because they have the legal right to be duped into inflicting harm or misery. This pay income is not particularly fortunate in terms of fortune. You must move your money around to pay various expenditures. You should not add to your debt or troubles by gambling, lending money to others, or taking guarantors.

This month's family horoscope is not favorable. You should pay greater attention to the health of the elderly and be cautious of mishaps that may occur to family members. You should also be aware of the risks associated with bereavement for older relatives. To avoid risk, turn on the burglar alarm when leaving the house.

The love horoscope predicts quarrels and disagreements. You should avoid attending places of amusement if at all feasible since this will foster division. In terms of health, avoid air allergies and other allergens. Be wary of the hazards of driving on the road. This month is not ideal for starting a new career, buying stocks, or making other investments.

Support Days: 3 Oct., 7 Oct., 11 Oct., 15 Oct., 19 Oct., 23 Oct., 27 Oct., 31 Oct.
Lucky Days: 12 Oct., 24 Oct.
Misfortune Days: 1 Oct., 13 Oct., 25 Oct.
Bad Days: 4 Oct., 6 Oct., 16 Oct., 18 Oct., 28 Oct., 30 Oct.

Month 10 in the Dragon Year (7 Nov 24 - 6 Dec 24)

This month, your fate will disturb the foundations of your life. Fortune's once-smooth road has gone up and down. Life is not as easy as it used to be. Anything you accomplish during this period seems as if your battery is weak and insufficiently charged. It will be quite tough to progress. However, it is simple to slip behind. This month, you should focus on controlling your mind and accomplishing any task. Before beginning, there should be communication and preparation with guidance. Take no chances. The completed work will not contain errors that you will have to go back and revise several times.

This paycheck fortune has enough money to get by. However, the money you hope to win from gambling or the windfall has a chance to win. You must face the risk yourself because it is not a large sum of money. Don't overinvest by mistake. Because the timing is off. You can run out of agents to withdraw your money. There are several challenges to overcome throughout this phase of labor. Many occupations have issues that need your constant intervention and resolution. However, you should prioritize resolving essential concerns first. Don't pause or contemplate too long. Being complacent is the same as abandoning the problem. It will just exacerbate the situation and prevent the task from being done. At this point, there is still serenity and comfort among the family.

It will be easy to fall in love. Even if you are trapped and have major challenges, your partner and loved ones will still aid and support you. However, the health aspect is not particularly favorable. This month, be wary of past ailments reappearing or the same pain sites reappearing. Also, be wary of lung illness, liver disease, heart disease, and diseases caused by excess.

Relatives and friends have faced problems and cannot be entirely trusted. You don't want to divulge anything just yet. Be cautious; there are still dishonest people out there seeking ways to damage you. When it comes to starting a new career, investing in stocks, and making other investments, you must preserve your heart and not be too greedy. Hoping to lose money by gambling with other people's money.

Support Days: 4 Nov., 8 Nov., 12 Nov., 16 Nov., 20 Nov., 24 Nov., 28 Nov.
Lucky Days: 5 Nov., 17 Nov., 29 Nov
Misfortune Days: 6 Nov., 18 Nov., 30 Nov
Bad Days: 9 Nov., 11 Nov., 21 Nov., 23 Nov.

Month 11 in the Dragon Year (7 Dec 24 - 5 Jan 24)

This month, the fate of persons born in the Year of the Dragon shifts toward partnership. As a result, we acquired the strength of others around us. You should never be apathetic when the Wheel of Fortune directs you. Accelerate work production, grow sales, and increase revenue. This month, you should do the following: Always cultivate and deepen positive relationships with individuals at all levels. Both must demonstrate their job potential to the best of their abilities. Dare to take on more demanding work, explore new chances in areas you were previously frightened of, or invest in a different business industry than you had intended. It was able to provide the all-clear to proceed fully. You will be able to broaden your career and earn more money.

In terms of employment, the route to prosperity veered off during this period. Your career will advance. The company will grow and flourish. You will also discover sponsors to help you along the road, double your success.

So, seize this excellent chance and make the most of it. This pay increase is a source of abundance. Money comes in from a variety of sources. The more attentive you are in accumulating wealth, the more money you will have. As a result, you should not be complacent and rush to make up for the months when your revenue was lower.

The family horoscope is serene. Examine how they interact with one another. It is a lucky moment to be in love. Whether it's asking for love, proposing, being engaged, or marrying. No worries about health; everyone is physically and psychologically robust. If ties between family and friends are cordial, you will most likely meet new people who will progress from friends to acquaintances. In terms of beginning a new career, investing in stocks, and making other decisions. This month, fresh chances will emerge that are appropriate for investing or growing your career to progress.

Support Days: 2 Dec., 6 Dec., 10 Dec., 14 Dec., 18 Dec., 22 Dec., 26 Dec., 30 Dec.
Lucky Days: 11 Dec., 23 Dec.
Misfortune Days: 12 Dec., 24 Dec.
Bad Days: 3 Dec., 5 Dec., 15 Dec., 17 Dec., 27 Dec., 29 Dec.

Amulet for The Year of the Dragon
"Phra Sangkajai bestows wealth (Smiling Buddha)"

This year, those born in the Year of the Dragon should set up and revere sacred things. Placing "Phra Sangkajai bestows wealth" on your work desk or cash register to pray for His might and prestige to assist in providing happiness. Having good fortune can provide good fortune and help remove misfortunes, change bad situations into positive ones, and promote careers and enterprises to advance, thrive, and make money.

A chapter in the Department of Advanced Feng Shui discusses the gods who will come to stay in the mia keng (house of destiny) for the yearly rounds, gods who can bring both good and terrible things to the god of fate in that year. In this scenario, it is vital to worship and boost your fortune by the gods who visit your birth year. It is said to produce the finest effects and have the most impact on you. To relied on that god's power to protect him when his fortunes declined and his miseries were lessened. At the same time, you should pray for blessings to help your business run smoothly, fulfill your wishes, and bring you and your family success.

Those born in the year of the Dragon or Mia Keng (house of fate) belong to the zodiac sign Sing. This year, your horoscope corresponds to your zodiac year. Furthermore, there are a lot of unfortunate stars in the horoscope. There have been things that have bothered you all year. Be wary of disagreements with people and probable treachery. There is a chance of losing riches in terms of fortune. Be cautious while investing and developing your business. It is possible, but you must increase the tightness.

The love story is still in the works. Long-distance travelers must be cautious of mishaps. Also, be cautious of thieves toward the end of the year. If you want to solve an issue, you should surround yourself with sacred things and wear auspicious pendants. "Phra Sangkajai bestows wealth" to request His Majesty's strength and prestige to aid safeguard and protect from harm and spread His reputation to be tranquil and joyful. The task being done is making progress and prospering. Money comes in and grows, providing the Lord of Destiny peace and contentment.

"Phra Sangkajayana" or "Phra Mahakajayana" was previously a highly lovely Buddha. She also has fair skin. It captivates both men and women who see it in general. As a result, it is a significant impediment to your Dhamma teaching. This is because some listeners got captivated by his outward appearance rather than paying attention to the Dhamma he preached. To overcome this hurdle, he hoped that his body would become fat and plump, leading spectators to lose interest in his lovely appearance.

Instead, he regarded his new shape as a symbol of perfection and luck. The arahant Phra Sangkajai bestows good fortune, knowledge, and compassion. Chinese and Thais of Chinese heritage are extremely religious. It is thought that adoring and bringing the Lord Buddha into one's house or office would result in three favorable outcomes for oneself and one's family: 1. Bringing prosperity and abundance 2. imparting beauty and charm 3. Increase one's intelligence and sharpness by bestowing wisdom.

Those born in the Year of the Dragon should also wear auspicious jewelry. "Phra Sangkajai bestows wealth" to wear around your neck or bring with you when traveling both close and far from home. Prosperity and growth in commerce and trade are required for the owner of his destiny to be filled with money and auspicious places. All year, the family is tranquil and joyful. It generates greater and faster efficiency and effectiveness than previously.

Good Direction: Southeast, West, and North
Bad Direction: Northwest
Lucky Colors: Red, Pink, Orange, White, and Yellow.
Lucky Times: 07.00 – 08.59, 15.00 – 16.59, 17.00 – 18.59.
Bad Times: 01.00 – 02.59, 05.00 – 06.59, 19.00 – 20.59.

Good Luck For 2024

Made in the USA
Las Vegas, NV
05 January 2024